I do not remember what's inside anymore

poems by

Veronica Tyler

Finishing Line Press
Georgetown, Kentucky

I do not remember
what's inside anymore

ACKNOWLEDGMENTS

To my husband. The steady heart at the center of all this undoing and
beginning again, and to the beauty that waits after breaking.

Publisher: Leah Huete de Maines
Editor: Christen Kincaid
Cover Art: Søren Daum
Cover Design: Elizabeth Maines McCleavy

Order online: www.finishinglinepress.com
also available on amazon.com

Author inquiries and mail orders:
Finishing Line Press
PO Box 1626
Georgetown, Kentucky 40324
USA

Contents

To a life after Paris

Wal-Mart

I died in a Wal-Mart.
Aisle thirty-one,
between a mop and Pine Sol.

As long as the love remained,
so would the smell
of ammonia.

Nails down to the quick dug into
dry, detached skin.
I found a way to escape.
It took five months.

It is five years later
in my nightmares
I am trapped inside a Wal-Mart.
The fluorescent lights make me dizzy
as I search every corner for you.

An Analog of Trepidation

He
pulled me
close.

My throat fit
perfectly
in his hand.

Its grip was
warm and
tight.

I smiled,
it was a privilege
to be so close.

Do not forget,
you are an analog
of trepidation.

You will not
prosper
without me.

Remember it,
always, he said.
I haven't.

Recovery

I dropped a cigarette from the window
as we drove the 405.

Talk some sense to me, I repeated.

I'll never be
what you wanted,
with the pinned-up hair,
quiet and sweet.

Mine will grow long and wild.
Unkempt.

I'll hold your secrets,
infused to my core.
I'll want to bash your fucking head in.
You'll go on, wanting more.

The gory depth of you is mine.
I'll be the carnage.

Talk some sense to me.

The Blue Moose

I forgot about the fire,
out of the blue,
around the beginning,
above The Blue Moose.

And, while we never
discovered what started it,
I let the embers in
and inhaled the fumes.

Would a delicate
tumble on a low setting
rid the odor
of you?

Chatham Hall

A morose existence. Dolorous repose.
I had known it in that green house.
And then the brown.

Something intangible.
Lured into sadness.
At the age of six.

Looking for escape,
I wandered pavement and the park.
The molecules of my existence, corrupted.

I could not help it then.
I cannot help it now,
And still I try.

And when I think,
when I muster all that's there,
In my interior, I think back to a girl.

She sits on a stoop in Chatham Hall,
much older.
Unrecognized, it is not the first time,
she asks me in for a sweet tea.

Stargazing

I discovered it was February when
constellations would plan my year.

I decided to accept
influence of the cosmos.

Abundance and confidence, it read,
signifying the composition in my bones.

My season of life.
A cycle lasting twelve months.

I guess that's why it hurt all over
when you called me insane.

Pleasant Street

Stacked
on
top,
one over
another, and
bay windows
to survey the neighborhood
that peered into
two different
stories of
our mirrored existence.

Stacked
on
top,
at the corner of
Pleasant Street
above the
barber and the
Chinese takeout. The bustle of
business, designed
to smother the rebels.

Stacked
on
top,
with my ears
pressed to the door,
wondering if you'd ever
bring someone else
home.
Would I hear her
from my room?

I've never been in love

I've never been in love,
I scream.
I mean it,
but I told you,
when I calmed down,
it was a lie.

I was just angry,
a form of
defense.
But it's true.

I guess there was one time
twenty years ago.

Green eyes,
I remember.
A blue house, across from mine.

On nights like these,
I lay in wake,
wondering if I fucked it all up.
But I wanted this dollhouse.
It's just missing you.

The Last Night on Earth

Their sins are not of
the same weight
or character.

And, despite the need
to prove what they had
was worth sharing,
defying the odds,
it failed to provide
material nourishment
preceding the last night on Earth.

Because the world was no longer
beautiful or kind
and, instead, it hurt
and sequestered what had,
always,
secretly,
been ours.

Incognito

I was
considered.
That is what
mattered.

A choice,
an option.
A valuable puzzle piece of
calculation.

The bruises etched
into my bones
will hold proof that
I was once worthy.

Hysteria
is what they would've
diagnosed.
Psychosis.

I do not remember what's inside anymore

My heart is sheathed in concrete.
You cannot enter,
cannot see its fillings.

I designed it this way
on purpose.
I have carefully constructed.
a way to make you feel connected.

It has never been authentic.
I am always rehearsed.
A lie to conceal will
sometimes spill over.

There is only one who shares
the same ground as I
who has known me
wholly.

I'll never see you again,
I scream.
I'll never see you again,
I laugh.
I'll never see you again,
I cry.

Holograms May Closely Resemble the Real Thing

I cannot always be the muse.
At some point I must be mortal.
Feelings need satisfaction, nourishment,
and love.

When you are an object to be
pondered, it elicits
temporary fascination, meant to rust
as you continue to drip the
negative exposure
of your artificial understanding
of who I am all over.

Atlas Shrugged

I was reading Ayn Rand,
supposing the importance of selfishness,
and I realized you might like
what she had to say
about putting yourself first,
damning the consequences of others
because there have been many moments
in this marriage
where desires have raged
against my shores
of empathy.

It's hot to be married to a writer

Oppression lurked in my heart as you said,
I love that you're a writer,
it's hot to be married to a writer,
I hope you sell one of these books.

He thought he could quit his job
if I publish
one of these books
he doesn't know the title of.

That must be why I write,
in cyclical motions, I am
attempting to discern
what it is
that might give existence value
while you contemplate
if it might make you richer.

Empty Cradle

lemon, blue,
a denim hue.

a reflection of past wants,
a future you.

an infant,
a friend,
a retreat,
and an end.

lemon, blue,
a denim hue.

Her First Marriage

I am thinking about cycles
and what they mean,
if I can break a path towards
destiny.

My nightmares come
while I'm awake,
dreams of solitude,
of fleeting peace, away
from the mess I've made.

When my mother spoke of her early days,
she'd recall her first marriage,
how it was destined to break.

He was sterile, you know,
far too much weed, she'd say,
as my mottled eyes recount,
how we drift day by day.

A year was all it took,
she'd give and give,
and he'd take and take.
So, it ended, she moved upstate.

And now it's August's heat
and I sit and wonder,
can I do anything right?
Hobbling down a path she despised.

It's almost funny,
how nearly a month has passed
since I told her I no longer
want her in my life.

Yet, here I am,
mourning and crying,
as I watch the marriage I long for
slowly dying.

Are we bound by these cycles,
forever entwined?

The Pigeons and I

Ubiquitous in existence,
diseased and discarded,
I found community with the pigeons.

After a counselor had told me,
What do you mean you're depressed?
You dress like everyone else.

I supposed I used to fit in,
ignoring the boiling emotion inside me
because at least I wore a high-low skirt
and sang in the choir.

And as I pushed it further inside, the ailments grew
as did the rhythms that told me I would never be
good enough.

The closer it grew to the surface, the shinier I became to men
and then, as expected, the further they'd retreat
once the thrill became danger.

And my heart hardened once I realized
I was just like the pigeons,
whose penchant for carrying disease would
eventually be too much
to keep in the home.

As it crumbles, I consider that

I think I'm having a midlife crisis
at twenty-six,
toiling as I write poems,
to call myself a poet,
silent and detached.

I am missing something
crucial, about love,
the way apocalypse teases,
leaves a yellow hue.
I get drunk at night.

Conforming for uncertainty,
a plan, ascension,
without the circumstance
of my echo, desire.
I never looked for exaltation.

I am laughing, reality detached,
the sound of gunshots,
and a political commentator
tells me things will be better,
now. The prospects of end.

If it's true,
will they come, take us,
or leave us black, blue?
Desecration for what is ancient, new.
Will we earn the savior? Red, white, and blue.

Would I finally be seen?

If I ended this here
and ran somewhere else,
Florida,
Arizona,
Oregon,
would it resolve this undeniable pain?

I have tried to do
things
the way I was taught.
Followed the book.
Referenced notes in the Appendix.

I have failed to
understand
why
this has consumed me
since I was six.
It comes
in waves.

If I left
this place
right now,
ran,
hid,
do you think,
finally,
suddenly,
I would be seen?

Veronica Tyler is the pen name of an Appalachian-based author and poet, and former magazine columnist. Her work focuses on blending imagination with interpretation. Her debut novella, *Paris*, released in 2024.

www.ingramcontent.com/pod-product-compliance
Lightning Source LLC
Chambersburg PA
CBHW022108080426
42734CB00009B/1521